HOW TO WORK FROM HOME BEING A MOM

DO YOUR WORK FROM THE COMFORT OF YOUR HOME, LEARN EVERYTHING YOU HAVE TO DO TO BRING YOUR OFFICE TO YOUR ROOM

Jessy M. Brown

Table of Contents

Introduction

Whether you're tired of working outside the home or ready to earn extra money, the opportunities available to home-working moms can be incredible.

If you're holding back for fear that your skills aren't perfected enough to turn your dreams into reality, relax! Even women who lack titles or high-priced "professional skills" will find that there are many options for launching lucrative businesses from home. It is also possible to get real staff jobs by working for others outside a home office. Telework is becoming more common than you might think. You may even be able to sign up as a hired or self-employed worker in companies around the world.

The truth is that it is not necessary to have a specific ability to work at home.

There are solutions to overcome almost every obstacle that stands in your way. There's no reason to be discouraged!

Immersing yourself in the prospect of working from home can be an incredible decision for you and your entire family. However, it needs to be carefully examined. Working at home can be a wonderful experience, but it's not for everyone.

In this book, we will discuss the things you will need to consider in order to succeed at it. There are some ways to find out if working at home really suits your style and some benefits and dangers that it's smart to explore before moving forward to start a career at home.

Although there will be obstacles - especially for busy mothers with hectic schedules - there are ways to crush almost all of them. There are techniques, tips, and ideas for facing adversity head-on and winning that can help put you on the road to success.

One of the keys to a successful home business is selecting the right field to work in. However, the opportunities can be a little amazing. Exploring all options carefully and how they might fit into your personal lifestyle should be an absolute priority before selecting the way forward.

No matter if you are planning to become an entrepreneur of some kind or if you want to work as a freelancer, there are also some things to keep in mind. From getting the necessary training and finding work to setting up a home office, we'll discuss what you need to know to make your dreams of working at home a reality.

How do I know if working from home is for me?

You love the idea of being able to work at home and you like the idea of spending more time with your family, but you're not sure that this is the right path for you. Don't worry, you're not alone in your doubts. Almost every woman who has started a successful career at home has faced them. Still, it's smart to be sure.

Working at home requires a lot of dedication, discipline and patience. It's not for everyone, and that's perfectly fine. There are some things that should be carefully considered if you intend to become a working mom at home. Even if you are a stay at home mom, adding a career to the mix can make a bit of a difference. To make sure you're going in the right direction for you, it's important to review things such as finances, family support and your ability to cope with the prospect of working at home. Some mothers prosper in this situation, but others wither.

> ## ➢ *FINANCIAL POSITION*

If you are planning to leave a paid job to work at home, you should have good financial management. In most cases, it will take some time to set up a business or an independent company enough to replace an everyday job. Beyond the capital needed to start the business, you will also need a reserve fund to cover the start-up period.

The amount of money you set aside will depend on a number of factors, among them:

Understand how large your monthly contribution to the family budget is. Make sure your figure is covered for at least a few months. Three months may do the trick, but it's a conservative (and safer) option to shoot six to twelve months. Keep these figures separate from what you will need to give your company a fighting chance like success, too.

Establishing a home-based business may require some start-up capital. Beyond what is needed to cover the family, you will also want money for equipment, marketing, licenses, etc. A small business loan may work in some cases, but for many home operations, you'll be on your own with the start-up costs.

While business plans may not always be developed exactly on time, you have a good understanding of your particular company's anticipation period. You will want to make sure you have the money available to cover this period and continue to grow the business. Be realistic here.

If finances get in your way, consider seeking loans, activating a savings plan or simply working in your business part-time at first. There are ways to make your dream happen even if cash isn't available as quickly as you'd like.

➢ *FAMILY SUPPORT IS CRUCIAL*

Entering a work at home company without the support of a solid family for the idea can turn out to be a big mistake. If family members don't understand that work time is important or that work calls shouldn't be interrupted with loud rock'n' roll music from a teen's room, then an uphill battle will have to be fought.

To make sure your family is on board, ask yourself the following questions:

Have I discussed the idea thoroughly with all the members of the family? If he hasn't, he'll want to. Making sure that everyone who is old enough understands that the fact that you are at home does not mean that work hours are less important is vital to your chances of success.

Will older family members provide support during emergencies? Home-working mothers still need to attend meetings, meet deadlines or go out and make contacts. When there is a need for serious concentration, it is imperative to have someone who can intervene and take care of children and/or household chores.

Will family members help? Just because you work at home doesn't mean you can or should take care of everything. It will help you greatly if family members help with the chores and do their part to make sure everything in the home flows smoothly.

Working at home after being in the world can be a little difficult for an entire family. If you've been a stay-at-home mom, the challenges can be even greater. After all, everybody's used to having you there to help them.

Moving into a career at home means

that even if you are there, sometimes priorities will have to change focus. If your family is truly on board, you will have an advantage in any effort you pursue.

➢ *SELF-DISCIPLINE*

It won't matter at all how much money you've saved to get started or the support your family provides, if you can't motivate yourself, you're in trouble. Self-discipline is one of the most important traits to have when trying to start a career at home. This applies to distance workers who will be working full-time for companies as well as future employers.

To make sure you have what you need on this front, consider asking these questions and responding honestly and frankly:

Am I motivated? If you don't have the motivation and drive to get up in the morning and get to work, a home-based business will be on unstable ground from the beginning. While half the reward of working at home is being closer to the family, you will still have to operate with drive to enjoy success in business. Like raising your children, a career at home will require time, attention and a little serious care.

Can I set the hours and follow them? When you own the operation or are self-employed, you can set your own schedule. In fact, doing so can be a big help in ensuring that life is better balanced. Of course, you can go out early to play with children from time to time, but you will have to stick to life on a more or less regular basis.

Can I resist temptation? One of the questions that self-discipline can overcome is to resist the temptation to do things other than work during working hours. When no boss is breathing down your neck, it may be too easy to watch TV, play computer games, or even do household chores instead of performing work-related functions. Surrender to temptation too often and your company might not fly.

> ## *INSULATION MANAGEMENT*

Depending on the type of business you plan to pursue, you may find yourself a little isolated from other people. Computer-based careers, for example, can make you work at home and never go out and see people beyond the family for days on end. Although this is not a problem for many, it can drive some women crazy. Make sure you know your position on the issue before you go ahead with a career choice that could put you in this position.

If you want to deal with the potential problem of frontal isolation, there are a few things that can help. These include

This is a great way to get out of the house every week or month. In addition, it can help make sure your business gets its name.

Even if your business is computer-based, there is nothing wrong with accepting and soliciting local customers. This can get you out of the "office" from time to time and help you grow your business as well.

It can be extremely beneficial to plan after-hours activities that do not involve staying home. Even a trip to the park with the kids every few days can keep your sanity under control. Grocery races don't count!

Volunteering at your children's schools Even volunteering once a week, a month, or on every field trip you take can get you out of the house and help you get to know other people. It can also serve as a great way to show your children how much you want to be involved in their lives. After all, if the business is yours, a "boss" won't be able to say he can't take two hours off every Tuesday to lend a hand at a school.

Making the decision to work at home can be excellent. However, to make sure the move is right for you, take the time to carefully examine the ups and downs and answer questions about yourself and your situation honestly.

Benefits of working at home

Working at home isn't all sun and roses for long, but it can have some incredible benefits that many mothers wouldn't trade for the world. The potential benefits of making this decision can impact your financial life, emotional life and even the very relationships you love.

Some of the most notable benefits of working at home include:

- Saving money on daily expenses If you're going to leave a job to work at home, you'll have to make up the loss, but there are some instant savings you can feel. Home-working mothers often save a great deal of money on such things as childcare, travel expenses, lunches and even dinners. After all, it is much easier to make sure that a nightly meal is on the table if you are around during the day to see that this is so.

- While programming may vary depending on the business opportunity being pursued, many home-based moms find that they have much more time to spend with their families. Even as they work, they can simply see more of the family and participate more in their daily lives. This is a reward that can make the decision worthwhile.

- Keeping up with children, home and work will be difficult no matter what. However, doing so with a job outside the home can be a stressful nightmare. Moms who work outside the home may experience a drop in stress levels when they enter into the rhythm of "being there" to do things. For example, throwing clothes in the trash before starting a day's work can become natural. So, too, you can take the time to greet the little ones at a bus stop and so on.

- Personal Rewards It doesn't matter if

you launch a business that sells items through private parties or enter data entry on your own, when you test your successes they will really be yours. Creating even a modestly successful home business can be incredibly rewarding on a personal level.

- Flexible hours While some businesses will be more flexible than others, most home-working moms find that they are much more flexible in what they can and can't do than when they worked outside the home. This can be an incredible advantage for mothers who want to make decisions when they work, on what days and for how long they do it.

- Working at home can be very rewarding for women who give perspective a serious opportunity. The rewards of doing so can range from the financial to the very personal.

> **WATCH OUT FOR THE TRAP.**

Working at home can carry a number of

rewards that make the company worthwhile. Mothers can thrive in these circumstances because the situation gives them the best of both worlds.

As fantastic as working at home can be, there are some potential risks. Understanding what they are can prepare you to face them and win. Although not everyone will experience the same scams working at home, some of the more common problems that might arise include things like:

Some mothers who work at home have a bit of difficulty getting into the balance between career and personal life. Whether they spend too much time working or not enough, not achieving a balance can have the potential to lead to disappointment in one arena, in the other, or both.

Isolation As discussed earlier, some home careers can be a little lonely in the grand scheme of things.

Guilt While the idea of working at home

often means having more time for the family, work should also be on the list of priorities. This means that there will be times when moms will have to say no or go about their business, even when a three-year-old has a tantrum. The long and short part of this reality is that sometimes moms feel guilty for not being there, even when they are there.

In some areas of work, background noises in a home can be a little embarrassing and may even seem unprofessional. Talking on the phone with a client while a child has a seizure or a dog barks loudly in the background does not sound as professional as many would like.

The danger of working at home often lies in not being able to "leave" work at the end of the day. With this in mind, many mothers work at home and tend to exaggerate to their detriment. While this may be good for business, exhaustion can occur if someone works 24 hours a day and does not relax, relax and breathe once in a while.

While it is certainly nice to be able to get out of bed in the morning and "inform" the office, this can be a double-edged sword. It's too easy to be sitting in that robe at 6:00 p.m. on a normal Tuesday. This can have a negative impact on self-esteem.

Although the traps are very real, there are ways to face them and win. No matter the challenge, having a good plan to deal with the situation can make all the difference.

Overcome obstacles

While obstacles will stand in the way of any business, some of the obstacles to home business are a little different. There are ways to fight each and every one of them. When you have an arsenal of weapons at your disposal, you can clear the path to success.

These tips can be very effective in helping mothers face and overcome any obstacles that stand in the way:

While flexibility is important, it is also important to have a schedule that is followed regularly. When you get firm on your work hours and try to keep a schedule, it's easier to find a balance that works in your life.

Create a home office Even if it is a wardrobe that is rethought as your own, having a room with a door to which to retreat for business calls and serious work from the deadline can be a lifesaver. Of course, get the laptop so you can work in the living room while your family buzzes around you, but have a shelter to go to when you need it most. Doing this, by the way, can even help in your taxes, so it's smart from some points of view.

If you're going to be a mom who works at home with young children, it's imperative that you have babysitters or daycare in line for when it's needed most. It won't matter if your business is related to sales or service, there will be some days when you won't be able to be available to your family.

Assign homework If your children are older, a home-based business can become everyone's job. Assign children tasks and tasks that they can do to help them. These may include business-related functions or even simply putting children on the crockery service to free them until the end of nightly calls. A little work never hurts anyone or the children who help a family function well and learn valuable lessons along the way.

Concentrating on the Say "No" award for the third trip to the park during a sunny week can be difficult, but doing so can be important. When your kids see you working hard to

your family, they can learn by example. Installing a strong work ethic early on can put young people on their own path to success.

Aside from deadlines, it's important to get up and dressed for work, even if you're moving from bed to computer. This can help you feel better about yourself and keep you motivated and projecting successful vibrations into the process.

Opportunities for all

No matter if you've never worked a day in your life or if you're leaving a long-term job, there are opportunities that almost everyone can take advantage of. Working at home and succeeding at it doesn't mean you have to have a four-year degree, a ton of specialized skills or a bank full of money. What you need is a good idea and the momentum to achieve it.

There are a variety of opportunities for unskilled or low-skilled workers. Some of the options include things like:

Sales There are a variety of sales-related businesses that you can explore that will allow you to base your operations away from home. Many companies that rely on moms at home to sell their products will provide you with the training you need to succeed. It is also possible to buy in a franchise territory for certain products. Just make sure you can back up a product before you try to sell it. If they don't sell you, the customers won't be either.

Many of the mothers who live at home have made a living selling items through online stores or through virtual auction sites. Whether you create items yourself or do a lot of shopping for garage sales and real estate, this option is quite easy to explore. It can also be amortized with a lucrative part or with full-time income.

Data Entry If you can use a computer and type with any degree of accuracy, you will find a wealth of opportunities available for the skills you have. Even if you are not the best typist in the world, there are ways to perfect skill enough for this opportunity to work on your own to bear fruit. As more companies outsource functions such as data entry, many housewives are finding that this niche fits perfectly with them.

Telemarketing It is often possible to get freelance jobs and even in telemarketing companies that depend on home-based workers. This type of work will not require a highly specialized skill set. If you can speak clearly on the phone, get your message across and be pleasant in the process, you should be prepared.

Many working mothers at home stumble upon their own niche based on their own personal hobbies. Some home-based businesses that have emerged from unique ideas or products include such things as craftsmanship, online sales, custom clothing production with online storefronts, soap and candle making, and much more. Options are limited only by imagination.

Personal assistants Some work at home, mothers run errands for others, work in a virtual environment to take the load off office employees, and more. The field of personal assistant can be very interesting to explore both locally and online. The potential here is growing as more companies outsource and more employees are afraid to take time off to carry out their personal projects.

Home child care is a popular option for mothers who want their children to be in a homely, welcoming environment. This option may be excellent for a home-based business. As a mother, you have many of the skills already required for the job.

Writing If you can chain sentences with ease, opportunities are available for freelance writers. While you may lack some of the skills for certain jobs, there are projects that can be done by beginners. Many blogging jobs, for example, require "everyday" people to write. This means that only a good writing voice and basic skills are required.

You may need a degree or specialized training for this, but this field presents some unique opportunities. Reaching out to online tutoring students can be an excellent way to make a living and reap the benefits of working at home at the same time.

Some companies are turning to virtual call centers to manage their customer service. In many cases, these call centers hire home-based workers to handle the shifts of incoming calls. Although this type of work will require fixed hours, it can still provide the scheduling flexibility that parents often require. In addition, some call centers can offer real full-time work with benefits for telecommuters. This can be an advantage if you don't want to start your own business to work from home.

While short-term training and licenses are required for this field, many who enter this field realize that they can work at home most of the time.

Transcription For those who have a gift for the keyboard, this can be an incredible field to enter. With basic training, standard transcription work can be done at home. With a more in-depth course of study, higher-paid medical transcription contracts can also be obtained.

The opportunities to work at home are practically endless. With jobs ranging from those that never require you to leave the house to those that might have you out and about making sales calls on your own schedule, your options are not limited, even if your basic skill set turns out to be so.

Maximise your skills

While many home-based job opportunities do not require special degrees or advanced training, some skills may be necessary for better-paid jobs. Fortunately, there are a variety of places you can turn to to hone the skills you need to succeed without spending a fortune in the process.

Even if you choose a field that does not require special skills at all, it may be important to consider some courses to increase your business acumen. Learning about such things as basic accounting, record keeping, marketing and the legal establishment of a business can be important to the success of a home-based business in many cases.

Depending on the field you are interested in entering, these points of sale can be helpful in providing you with the right training quickly:

Local high schools often offer evening classes for their own students and community adults seeking to improve their skills. While the curriculum may include classes in standard high schools, many professional development programs are also offered. These can range from technical and typing classes to accounting and beyond. Don't worry, they won't make you take history and math again unless you want to!

Public technical schools can be invaluable resources for training in a variety of fields. Some of the programs that could be offered that could be of great use for a career at home include transcription, marketing, computer operation, basic accounting, and so on. These places are also known for offering high-tech courses. If, for example, you want to learn how to build websites, state or local technical schools are a good place to look for low-cost lessons.

Home certification courses can provide the skills and paperwork needed to start a career in the blink of an eye. Opportunities here may include things like medical transcription, accounting, marketing and more.

As more technical schools, colleges and universities take advantage of the power of the Internet to teach, course availability is increasing. While offers can vary greatly, students at home can do everything from learning how to use Microsoft Office products to getting a master's degree-everything from the comfort of their own home.

Field-based certification associations representing certain fields of work may offer certification or licensing training classes at low cost. Obtaining training to obtain a real estate license, for example, can take only a few months of study through a localized council of real estate agents.

Small Business Development Centers Located in many metropolitan areas, these government-funded agencies are known to host a variety of programs, workshops, and certification classes. These centers can also be incredible resources for establishing a business correctly to comply with local, state and federal regulations.

If you intend to sign with a franchise company or work in a territory as a home seller, training will be provided in many cases. Depending on the field or product you choose, the associated classes may cost you nothing at all. For example, sales-based companies that operate using home parties usually offer extensive, hands-on training. Many franchises, too, offer a variety of hands-on courses to help those who shop enjoy success.

On-the-job training Some freelance jobs will provide basic on-the-job training to contractors. Companies that hire distance workers to receive incoming calls, for example, may also offer training.

Getting the training that may be necessary for many home-based businesses is usually much easier than you might think. Go to the right place and the skills you have can be easily added.

Where to find a job?

Making the decision to work at home and select a field to follow will not be enough to get things moving. Unless you plan to build your own business from scratch, you'll need to know where to go to find jobs and opportunities in your home. There are a number of options that can be incredibly helpful to help you start earning money at home. However, there are a few things to watch out for. The world of work at home is not immune to swindlers, unfortunately.

✓ *EMPLOYMENT AGENCIES*

Local employment agencies can be an invaluable resource for the self-employed, semi-skilled workers and even for those seeking jobs in companies that put homeworkers on the payroll. To find an employment agency worth working with to boost your career, be sure to do so:

Define their interests: Employment agencies may be more specialized in the types of jobs they handle. Make sure your interests and the career area you plan to pursue are clearly defined to eliminate agencies that may not be able to help you.

Research agencies in your area: Once you know what you want to pursue and perhaps even what fields you want to stay away from, look for agencies in your area that have a reputation for helping people in your sphere of interest. If you can't get recommendations, call local agencies and ask what they handle.

Costs associated with research: Most employment agencies charge the employer, not the job seeker. Be sure to verify this before dealing with an agency. It's no fun getting a job just to discover that a cut will be removed from the top!

Employment agencies can be invaluable

resources for launching certain areas of interest in working at home. Make sure that if this is the path you want to follow, the agency you work with has experience in your area of specialization or interest.

✓ *THE FRANCHISES*

If you prefer not to invent the wheel to enjoy a home business opportunity, working with a franchise or signing with a sales company based in the territory can work perfectly. Both options can offer great advantages when it comes to backup and support, but there are things to keep in mind before signing on the dotted line. These include

Recognition: Whether you are buying from a franchise or simply representing a company through sales, make sure that the product and/or service is recognized and of good reputation. Even with growing or new businesses, it is feasible to test water. The fact that a company offers franchises for sale does not mean that its products or services are in great demand.

Level of support: If you are not entering the company with a lot of training, make sure the opportunity comes with a lot of support. Many franchise companies offer basic training in sales and business, for example. Sales companies, of course, should help you develop a plan to sell your products.

Your market: It won't do you any good to open the exact tenth franchise in a 20-block area. Make sure you understand your market and your needs. This also applies to the establishment of sales territories. Too much "friendly" competition and your chances of success could be greatly affected.

Associated costs: Make sure you have good management of the costs associated with taking this route. Some franchises are very affordable, but others can be incredibly expensive.

Your interests: It simply doesn't make

sense to set up a store with a company, product or service in which you have no interest. The effort is likely to plummet if you can't fully support it. Explore your interests closely and then match them with available opportunities.

Time involved: Some opportunities may sound very good until the amount of work involved is clearly understood. If you want to ensure that flexibility is maintained, it is imperative that you control what is really needed to succeed.

The franchise or sales route can be an easier way to get into a home-based business that has a real chance of success. However, in order to enjoy the results and rewards you crave, it is imperative that you first do some research.

✓ *GET JOBS THROUGH WEBSITES*

Harnessing the power of the Internet can be a great way to find work at home.

In the online arena, you'll find Web sites that can help you:

If you want a job at home, but at home, it makes sense to look for a number of companies around the world that are known for putting teleworkers on the payroll. This can make finding opportunities that pay much more easily.

There are a variety of Web sites that specialize in matching the self-employed in a number of fields with hiring employers. Although these are usually short-term positions, they can be very lucrative over time. This is especially true if short-term employers keep coming back for more. Freelance writers, for example, can connect with a variety of online employers and find more work than they can handle if they play their cards right.

If you like the idea of selling candles in a party atmosphere, for example, finding the right company to deal with can be a lot easier online. Here you'll discover a variety of sites that can connect you to the right opportunity.

Community sites Community-listed Web sites often have areas that connect home-based workers with possible actions. Although not all offers are legitimate, these sites may be worthwhile.

Some online employment agencies deal to a large extent with telework positions and other opportunities at home. They can offer an open door to finding short- and long-term employment opportunities in a variety of fields.

The options for connecting with potential employers in the online arena are almost endless. However incredible some of the opportunities may seem, it is imperative to be aware of some potential dangers.

✓ *THINGS TO AVOID*

As easy as some places can make it to find potential job opportunities at home, not all the ones out there are exactly reputable. With this in mind, it is important to avoid fraudsters by taking a cautious approach to any proposal. To avoid problems with home employment opportunities, independent contracts and more, be sure to do so:

Don't sign to sell products for a company without understanding exactly what those products are and what the company's reputation is. If you're self-employed, investigate the employer's reputation. Independent sites, for example, often offer feedback ratings. For other business opportunities, check with local chambers of commerce or the Better Business Bureau for background information.

Many ads for home workers offer a ton of money for a little work. Others will try to charge you for the opportunity to work for them. Unless it's a franchise with a participation fee, be very careful of anyone who tries to get your money so you can make money. Also, if the work at home sounds too good to be true, it probably isn't. Exercise common sense here and look at the backgrounds.

Contracts of use It may be too easy for the self-employed, for example, to slip on this front. Make sure you get customers under contract, even if it's for just one job in the very short term. This protects not only you, but also the independent employer.

If your idea is to work at home most of the time and enjoy a flexible schedule, don't sign up for a home sales stall that will eat up to 80 hours a week. Consider all of your goals as you explore the possibilities that exist.

Finding employers for many positions in the home is not as difficult as it seems. There are a number of resources that can make the task quite easy.

Some advice...

While not all home-based jobs will require interviewing or proposal creation skills, many will. If you have decided that you would like to work for a company that hires employees at home or with a local contract, for example, you will want to improve your interviewing skills. If you are thinking of becoming self-employed via the Internet, you will need to know how to present yourself in the best possible way through proposals.

• *GETTING INTERVIEWS*

If you haven't interviewed for a position before or it's been a long time, there are some tips that can help you put your best foot forward. To make sure you do your best in any interview situation:

Although it may not be necessary to wear a straitjacket and high heels for every interview, dress neatly, cleanly, and professionally. First impressions do matter.

Be prepared to answer a variety of work-related and other questions. Understand the position, the company, and what your role might be before you walk through the door. In addition, it is a good idea to prepare for anything that may be thrown in your path. Plan a personal interview, but don't lose your cool if it turns out to be a panel. Just breathe and be yourself.

Make eye contact This is essential to send the right message to potential employers. This can help you earn a reputation for trust, competence and honesty - everything employers look for even in home-based workers.

While you may not need a home office or a good computer setup before getting a job, having plans in place can give you the advantage of the initiative you need.

Try to be as relaxed and safe as possible during any job interview. This will help you answer questions in greater depth and can also help you make a good impression. Even if the position is your "dream", don't panic thinking it will be the end of the world if you don't get it. This will undermine confidence and probably give you a tense appearance.

Don't be afraid to bring your qualifications, experiences and strengths to the forefront. Remember, an interview is really a sales situation. Instead of a product or service, you will try to sell yourself. Do the job well and you'll get the job.

Don't try to make yourself look like you're more than you are. Be honest in answering questions. If you don't know something, admit it. Emphasize that you are willing and able to learn anything you can think of.

Be realistic Make sure you are at least

reasonably qualified for a position. If the job requires highly specialized skills and you don't have them, it's probably unrealistic to go after the job.

Face-to-face interviews can be quite stressful, but there are ways to do it. The more prepared and relaxed you are, the better you will find potential employers. This can give you the edge you need to outperform the competition.

- ## *YOUR FIRST ONLINE INTERVIEW*

Interviewing or applying for a job in a virtual environment can be a little more complicated. While some positions may also include a face-to-face interview, many do not. This means that you will often have to sell yourself based solely on credentials and written communications. There are some tips that may help you perform here. These include

Since it is very likely that you will have to land the work only with written materials, it will be imperative that the proposals are presented correctly. Be sure to take the time to update your resume and qualifications, review your proposal, and offer only what you can really offer. If you are planning to work on your own, keep your offer prices competitive.

Some independent employers prefer to interview candidates by telephone or in chat rooms. Make sure you are available to talk when needed.

Once proposals are submitted, it may be a good idea to follow up with a potential employer and be available to answer any questions. If you are bidding through a freelance matching service, this may not be possible, but in other areas it may be a valuable habit to get into.

Interviewing for a full-time job or even for a freelance contract can be a bit overwhelming. The more prepared you are for what you can expect, the better your performance will be. With a little confidence, you'll make good things happen for yourself.

- ### *SET UP THE HOME OFFICE CORRECTLY*

Whether you intend to be self-employed, make sales, buy a franchise or telework for a full-time employer, you will find that having a home office is a very important consideration. Even if it's just a closet with its own privacy door, having a retreat can be very important for productivity levels and even sanity.

You'll probably find that you don't have to spend a small fortune to set up a home office. Even with a relatively low budget, you can get the tools you need for almost any professional field. The basics to consider include:

A workstation Even if you use two file cabinets with a desk stretched over them, having a place to place other materials and distribute the paperwork can be very smart.

File cabinet(s) It is okay if these are part of the "desk" or if they are standing on their own. Either way, you're going to need them to keep important files, such as customer information, purchase receipts for the business and so on.

A computer This is the bread and butter for many businesses in the home. A reliable computer with the right office software can even help with a sales-based franchise. It's also a good idea to have a high-speed Internet connection. This is especially true if you plan to work as a freelance or virtual teleworker.

A phone Having a dedicated business phone line is a great idea. Even if you don't want to do this at first, consider at least putting a phone in the office.

Printer/fax/scanner To keep costs down, a combined unit can work very well.

A planner. You're gonna do a lot of juggling. To keep up with all of this, it's smart to have a calendar or scheduler to help you schedule your days.

Don't forget to stock up on other supplies you may need, such as pens, paper, log books, files, invoices, business cards, etc.

Establishing a home office is a very good idea to give you the space you need to do your job. Even a very basic configuration can help tremendously.

The road to success

Unless you've decided to work remotely for a company, there are some things you'll want to do to get yourself on the road to success. Selecting a business field to follow, setting up a home office and even getting a little training will not be enough to build a list of clients and keep them coming back for more.

Whether you intend to open a sales franchise or freelance for a hired employer, there are several other moves you need to make to get off to a good start. Advertising, networking, and building and protecting your reputation will become important considerations once you are immersed in the work at home.

✓ *WHY ADVERTISING IS IMPORTANT*

Just because you've decided to do

business on your own doesn't mean customers will start knocking on your door. Advertising is essential for franchises, sales in the territory, online sales and even for the self-employed. People simply need to know who you are and what you offer before they are interested in your products or services. Hanging a sign isn't enough.

So how can you get the information you need about your new home-based business? These advertising modes can help people get to know you and your business:

Depending on what you are going to do, print advertising can be a good way to do it. If you plan to sell products in a particular area, for example, local newspapers can do wonders. If you want to offer your services as a virtual assistant for small businesses, specialist journals can give you a boost.

Pay per click online advertising and

other search engine driven online ads can work very well to get you online sales sites, names of freelancers and much more circulating on the Web. It can also be a very good idea to set up your own site even for a highly localized business.

Free advertising One of the best ways to get at least an initial boost is to enjoy the benefits of free advertising. If you are opening a franchise or territory sales business in your community, send a press release to the local media. If you are going to do business online, consider writing a blog about your experience or field to generate traffic to your website. You can also write guest columns for others, agree to be interviewed by an online writer, or issue web-based press releases to tell who you are and what you do.

Other forms of advertising Television, direct mail, radio and other advertising tools can work well, depending on your budget and the type of business you're in.

Consider your options carefully, however, as these modes of getting the word out could cost more than you want to pay as a start.

Opening a business is not enough to ensure success. Once you're ready to get started, your potential customer base will need to know about you. Advertising is essential to drive traffic and business your way.

✓ *THE PURPOSES OF NETWORKING*

Networking is really another form of advertising, but it is one that can be quite affordable and effective. When you get in touch, you're basically becoming the best seller for your business. In addition, this can get you out of the house by doing something very important to build your sales and reputation.

Networking options are a little more extensive than many people think. Some opportunities that might be worth exploring include:

Local chambers of commerce Local chambers of commerce provide an excellent platform for anyone selling a product or service to spread the word. While cameras can consume a little time in the grand scheme of things, they offer valuable training in exchange for membership costs and can help business owners and freelancers enjoy a way to become a valuable part of a community.

Many communities have their own networking groups that offer less in the form of programs and more in the form of face-to-face time with other business owners who may be looking for products or services. Networking groups can meet weekly, monthly or quarterly. In some areas, you will find general networking groups and even those aimed at working with mothers.

Online Options If you intend to sell products online or want to work as an independent data entry professional, you will find that Web networking can be very important to your success. To spread the word about what you do, consider joining online contact groups, writing guest or expert articles for websites, etc. Launching a blog for self-promotions can also work very well for traffic and interest your way. Using social networking sites can also be an interesting and effective way to create a rumor about your business.

Sponsorships Launch a sales franchise in a local community and start the first day sponsoring an event, sports team or something similar can spread goodwill instantly. Sponsorships do not necessarily have to be expensive to be effective. If you are entering an online business, your options may be limited.

Networking is not only a vital advertising vehicle for your business, but can also serve as a good "distraction" for you. As a working mom at home, you'll find that going out and promoting your business is fun, rewarding and offers a very enjoyable change of pace.

Opening a business without anyone knowing you're there isn't smart. There are a variety of ways you can spread the word about who you are and what you do. To get the most out of marketing, consider a multifaceted approach.

✓ REPUTATION IS EVERYTHING

Whether you plan to sell products at home parties, open a franchise, or contract work is your specialty, you'll need to protect your reputation zealously. Building a good reputation and the benefits of doing so will have a very positive impact on the success of your business.

Your reputation can impact your business and your referrals. If you build great relationships with customers, your business will typically be successful. If you don't, you might fall.

To make sure your reputation is stellar, make sure you do:

Keep your word. Just promise what you can keep and do exactly that. This will help you build trust with customers. In turn, it can lead to repeat business and word-of-mouth advertising for your products or services.

Treating customers with respect Customer service is the key to building lasting business relationships. Treat potential customers with respect and courtesy and this will pay off.

Make sure products or services are on par. Although your professionalism will help you get off on the right foot, it is your products or services that will continue to sell your business. Make sure they offer quality and value and customers will keep coming back.

Mothers can establish lucrative and

successful businesses. If you take the right steps to plan your business, disseminate information and provide services, your efforts should be worthwhile.

What about my benefits? Where are they?

Your task is done, you have selected your business and you are ready to go full speed ahead. Just when you think you've got it all planned out, a friend asks you how you'll compensate for those valuable benefits your current employer provides.

So *how do you respond? Can you fill in the gaps?*

Most likely it can be adequately covered. From health insurance and retirement to savings, you'll find that it's often possible to recreate roughly the same type of coverage you enjoyed as a full-time employee in the rat race. The right approach to take will depend on your personal circumstances.

> ➤ *TAKE OUT INSURANCE*

If medical, dental, and vision coverage are concerns, home-working mothers generally have options available to them. Making sure your family is covered should, of course, be a high priority. These are the most common options open to homeworkers:

If your spouse can get job insurance that covers the whole family, this may solve the problem completely. There are also some benefits to following this route. Although private insurance policies can be had and are not as expensive as many think, they tend to be quite limited in coverage. Employers' PPOs and HMOs will cover more and usually no exclusions.

Unless there are important pre-existing conditions to deal with, it is possible to purchase private HMO and PPO policies to cover the family. Look carefully for coverage and costs should not bankrupt. Be aware of the limitations of each particular policy you see. Policies that are not group policies tend to have many restrictions and "small print" that must be considered closely.

Group If your new home-based business will employ more people than just you, you may qualify for group insurance coverage. This means that you will have access to the same type of coverage options that an employer would provide. The costs of this can vary greatly, but it may be worth considering if you have workers and a whole family to cover.

Insurance is simply an obstacle that stands in the way of self-employment. Explore your options carefully and you'll be able to find a solution that works. Keep in mind that costs can vary greatly. It is worth checking all avenues and choosing a final route that provides the best coverage for the lowest possible investment.

> ### *AND YOUR RETIREMENT?*

Although insurance is a great consideration, it should not be forgotten about the future either. If you're leaving a job that offers retirement benefits or savings vehicles, you'll want to find ways to duplicate or even improve the tools at your disposal. You can lose that corporate match by flying solo, but you can make sure you save for your retirement as a freelancer.

Some of the options available to help stay-at-home moms save nest eggs for their golden years include:

These retirement savings accounts can help you protect your tax savings as you build for the future. IRAs have contribution limitations, but can be a valuable tool to use as part of a general retirement plan.

401ks This is another vehicle for retirement savings. The problem with 401ks is that they tend to be linked to the stock market, which means they can cope with dramatic ups and downs. It may not be smart to use a 401k as the only option, but they can serve as a good table in a plan.

Bonds Although their earnings are not necessarily dramatic, they can turn out to be quite solid investments. Federal and municipal bonds can be rewarded with good long-term rewards.

Stocks Be careful when using a portfolio as the only option due to possible ups and downs. Still, it's a table worth considering.

Other investments Gold, real estate and other tangible investments can be considered part of a long-term investment package.

One of the potential drawbacks of working at home is a lack of retirement funds. You can overcome this obstacle if you plan carefully and make sure you save for your future.

➢ *EVERY PENNY COUNTS*

Retirement savings are important, but so are short-term savings. If you plan to help nurture your family's lifestyle or even finance it entirely, saving cash for a rainy day is a smart thing to do. This is also a great way to prepare for the downtime that can occur with any business.

Some of the options worth exploring on the savings front, many of which are mentioned for retirement investments. Stocks, bonds and other investments can pay off.

For simpler savings, you can consider things like:

Traditional Savings Open a savings account and start saving a fixed amount every week, every other week, or every month. Keep at it and your savings will build up over time.

Money Market Accounts If you want to earn a little more interest on your money, these can work very well. They work like normal checking or savings accounts, but earn more interest.

Making a living as a good stay at home

mom is certainly possible, but it may not be enough to cover your long-term bases. If you want to protect your income, your health and your future, it's wise to make adaptations for insurance, retirement and standard savings.

Conclusion: How to manage everything and not fall in the attempt?

If you think working at home will be "easier" than any other option available to you, chances are you're cheating yourself. It's different, more convenient, immensely rewarding, but not necessarily a walk in the park. You can learn to manage everything and excel in your personal and professional life.

To make sure you juggle your work, family, and domestic responsibilities as easily as possible, it may be helpful to consider the following tips, techniques, and strategies for doing it all:

This particular piece of advice cannot be emphasized enough. If you plan to work a full eight-hour day from morning to afternoon or if you intend to work at night after the children go to bed, set your schedule and try to stick with them.

Take advantage of downtime If you have some downtime during the set hours, take advantage to do other things on your plate. Do some housework, hang out with the kids, make dinner or just relax a little.

Even working at home, it's very likely that you won't be able to handle it all every day inside and out. Give yourself permission to let the house go a little bit in favor of getting a big contract or buying enough time to take the kids to the park. Prioritize what's really important and your juggling act will work.

If you've never worked at home before with kids running around, you're about to embark on a patience exercise. Your children may not initially understand that they can't interrupt every five minutes. You will have to learn the fine art of compromise and even how to be firm and loving to accomplish this. With a little effort, you can avoid hurting small egos.

Launching a stay-at-home business can make some things in life a lot easier. It may also present a new set of challenges. Be prepared to prioritize what matters and engage on points that are not so important. If you do these things, you can juggle everything and keep your business going, your sanity intact and your family in top form.

➤ *A FEW WORDS OF FAREWELL*

Choosing to be a working mom can be one of the best decisions you will ever make. With a little planning, patience and effort, you can spend more time with your family while earning a living in the process.

While working at home can be a big challenge, the rewards can be worth it. To make sure you have your bases covered before you dive into this decision, don't forget to do so:

Whether you're teleworking for a full-time employer or starting your own business, working at home is not for everyone. Be sure to really explore the possible ups and downs of the decision. It's okay to decide that this option isn't for you.

Select the right field You don't have to have an Ivy League title to make an incredibly successful career as a stay at home mom. However, you need to choose the career opportunity that best suits your interests and the skills you have or can gain. Make sure that the company you plan to start really keeps your interest.

If your family isn't behind the decision, you might have a hard start. Have frank and open discussions about what you hope to do and what that means for the whole family. Having him at home is more likely to be worth any sacrifices other family members may have to make.

Set your parameters Set up a home office, set work hours and get ready to start on the right foot. Doing these things can help you build and maintain a professional image even if you're wiping the slime off your shirt while talking to a customer on the phone! The best part is that the customer won't be able to see what you're doing!

If you're not going to work for someone else full time, be sure to spread the word about your business. Be sure to inform your friends, family, and co-workers. Pay attention to advertising, networking and other viable options to attract customers. Continue to cultivate advertising business opportunities after your launch to keep your business in the public eye.

Cover your bases Don't overlook the importance of insurance, retirement savings and a rainy day fund. Plan ahead how to handle these things and save them for emergencies and the future will become a habit that your whole family can live with.

Relax Work at home is a juggling act. There's no denying that. Some days will be better than others. Just relax and do your best every day. If you sweat the little things, you'll go crazy.

Becoming a stay at home mom is an amazing way to combine the most important job of your life with the second most important. If you plan carefully and prepare for some ups and downs along the way, the rewards of leaving the day-to-day world to stay at home will quickly accumulate and keep coming.

Just remember that everything will not happen overnight and that it will take time before you see a change in your life for the better.

Now yes, I wish you the best in your results, and remember, everything is practical; theory without action is of no use to you. It brings everything you learn into real life.

A big hug, your friend, Jessy!

By the way, when you achieve your results little by little, I highly recommend you, if you want to learn much more about methods of making money, the book of a great author from whom I learn a lot, on "SECRET STRATEGIES TO MAKE A LOT OF MONEY IN THE MULTINIVEL BUSINESS", is a book that I am sure will help you a lot on your way to "financial freedom".

Without further ado, you can find it in the Amazon search engine, such as: "Secret strategies to earn a lot of money in the multi-level business" or looking for its name, such as: "Gaston Echevarria"... Once again I wish you success in your results!